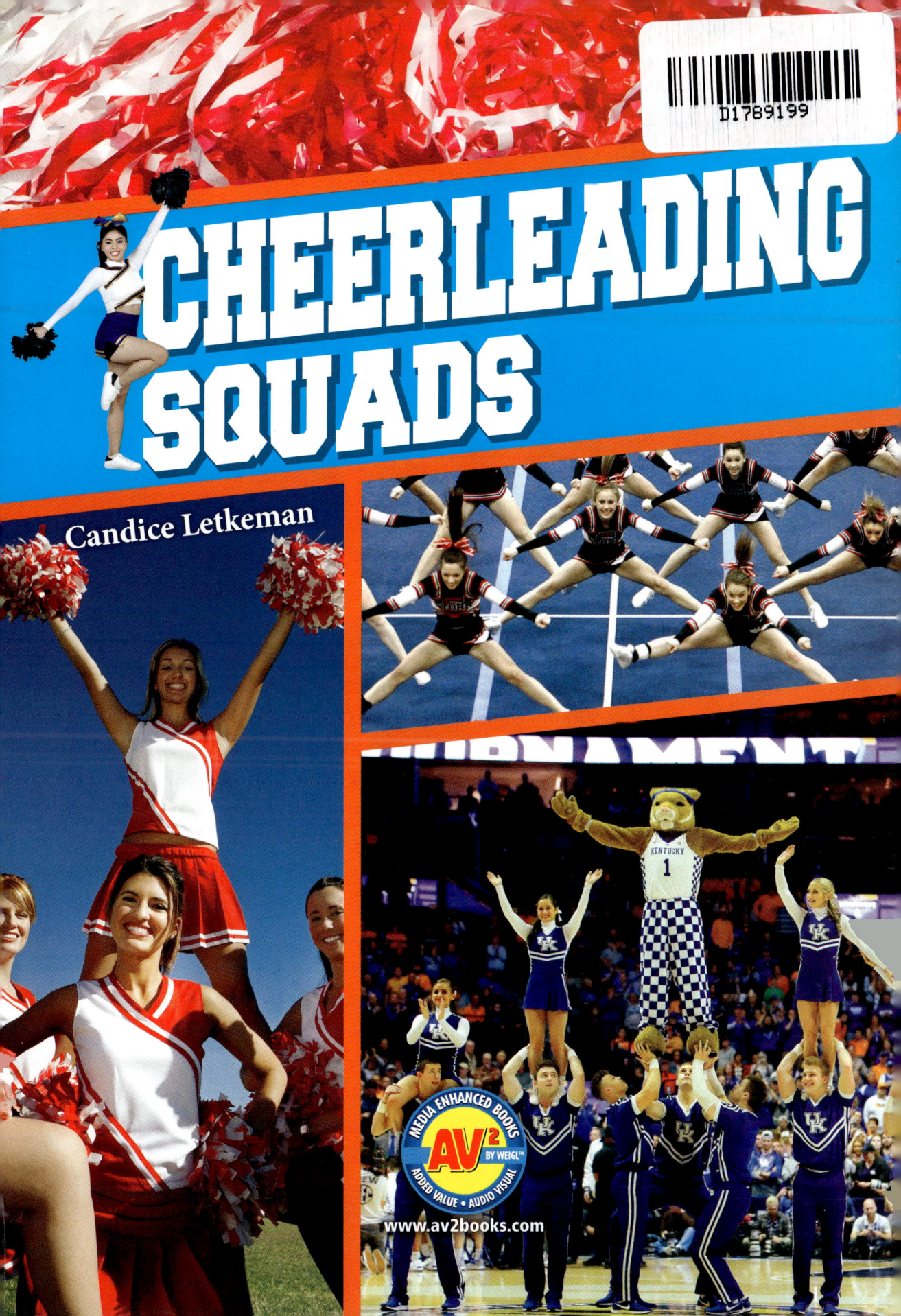

CHEERLEADING SQUADS

Candice Letkeman

MEDIA ENHANCED BOOKS
AV² BY WEIGL™
ADDED VALUE • AUDIO VISUAL

AV² provides enriched content that supplements and complements this book. Weigl's AV² books strive to create inspired learning and engage young minds in a total learning experience.

Your AV² Media Enhanced books come alive with...

Audio
Listen to sections of the book read aloud.

Key Words
Study vocabulary, and complete a matching word activity.

Video
Watch informative video clips.

Quizzes
Test your knowledge.

Embedded Weblinks
Gain additional information for research.

Slideshow
View images and captions, and prepare a presentation.

Try This!
Complete activities and hands-on experiments.

... and much, much more!

Go to **www.av2books.com**, and enter this book's unique code.

BOOK CODE

AVC99737

AV² by Weigl brings you media enhanced books that support active learning.

Published by AV² by Weigl
350 5th Avenue, 59th Floor
New York, NY 10118
Website: www.av2books.com

Library of Congress Cataloging-in-Publication Data
Names: Letkeman, Candice, author.
Title: Cheerleading squads / Candice Letkeman.
Description: New York, NY : AV2 by Weigl, [2020] | Series: Cheerleading |
  Includes index. | Audience: K to Grade 3.
Identifiers: LCCN 2019014389 (print) | LCCN 2019016817 (ebook) | ISBN 9781791110000 (Multi User ebook) |
  ISBN 9781791110017 (Single User ebook) | ISBN 9781791109981 (hardcover : alk. paper) | ISBN 9781791109998
  (softcover : alk. paper)
Subjects: LCSH: Cheerleading--Juvenile literature.
Classification: LCC LB3635 (ebook) | LCC LB3635 .L47 2020 (print) | DDC 791.6/4--dc23
LC record available at https://lccn.loc.gov/2019014389

Printed in Guangzhou, China
1 2 3 4 5 6 7 8 9 0 23 22 21 20 19

052019
103118

Project Coordinator: Heather Kissock
Designer: Ana Maria Vidal

Every reasonable effort has been made to trace ownership and to obtain permission to reprint copyright material. The publishers would be pleased to have any errors or omissions brought to their attention so that they may be corrected in subsequent printings.

Weigl acknowledges Getty Images, Shutterstock, and Alamy as its primary image suppliers for this title.

CHEERLEADING SQUADS

Contents

AV² Book Code.. 2

The World of Cheerleading Squads 4

History of Cheerleading Squads 6

Cheerleading Squads Timeline............... 8

How Cheerleading Squads Work............ 11

Cheerleading Squads Athletes
and Coaches 12

The Right Tools 14

The Right Moves 16

Getting Involved.................................... 18

PROFILE: Prospect High Panthers 20

Quiz 22

Key Words/Index.................................... 23

Log on to www.av2books.com 24

The World of Cheerleading Squads

Cheerleading squads are full of energy and excitement. These groups of cheerleaders cheer on sports teams. They perform entertaining routines. Some squads do **stunts**, too.

There are about 400,000 cheerleaders on high school squads in the United States.

Many schools have cheerleading squads. This includes colleges. **Professional** squads cheer at professional sports games. Football and basketball teams have cheer squads. **All-star** squads do not cheer at games. They go to competitions.

Cheer squads are like other sports clubs. Members work together. They learn and practice together. Cheerleaders get to know each other well. Often, a squad feels like a family. Its members trust each other. This way, they perform their best at all times.

Most squads have between **5 and 36** athletes.

More than half of all cheerleaders are between **7 and 17** years old.

Early cheerleading squads called out chants and did simple motions.

History of Cheerleading Squads

The first squads cheered for college teams. They began cheering at football games in 1898. By the 1960s, squads were cheering at basketball games, too. Squads first cheered at women's professional sports in 1973. Today, squads also cheer at soccer and volleyball games. They attend other sports as well. This includes wrestling.

In the United States, more than 120,000 cheerleaders are on All-star squads.

The first squads were all male. This lasted for more than 30 years. Women did not begin cheerleading until 1923. Later, World War II (1939–1945) started. Many men went to fight. Women joined squads in large numbers. By the 1960s and 1970s, cheerleading squads were almost all female. Cheerleading competitions began in the 1980s. Competitive squads included both males and females.

Cheerleading spread to high schools by the 1960s, too. College squads taught high school students basic cheerleading skills. Today, almost every high school across the country has cheerleading squads.

All-star cheerleading began in the late 1980s. It helped cheerleading grow even more. Today, there are almost 4 million cheerleaders in the United States.

Cheerleading Squads Timeline

The first squads had only a few members. Cheerleaders did simple cheers and motions. Now, there are squads at all levels. Many cheerleaders do advanced stunts and take part in large competitions.

By the 1950s, most U.S. colleges had cheerleading squads.

1954 The Baltimore Colts form the first professional squad. The squad has 10 members. It often performs with the Colts marching band.

1973 The Pop Warner program adds cheerleading. Many levels are included. These squads learn **sideline** cheerleading.

1982 The first All-star squad forms. The squad is called the Q94 Rockers. It is from Richmond, Virginia.

2015 The University of Kentucky cheer squad sets a record. It wins eight national **championships** in a row.

2016 The TV show *Cheer Squad* starts. It follows the Great White Sharks squad. The squad comes in third in the world championships.

2018 The Team Finland All Girls Premier squad wins **Worlds**. Finland is the first team to ever beat the United States in this competition.

School squads might practice for two to three hours each time they meet.

How Cheerleading Squads Work

Cheerleading squads are formed during **tryouts**. Many tryouts last for three days. Cheerleaders practice in groups for the first two days. Coaches then judge the cheerleaders on the third day. Some coaches give cheerleaders points for skills used in jumps and **tumbling**. The cheerleaders with the most points make the squad.

School cheerleading squads practice often. They meet between three and five times a week. The focus is usually on specific skills. Squads also practice the cheers and routines they will perform at games.

Many school squads lead the crowd in cheering at games. They cheer from the sidelines during the game. They use chants and signs to help the crowd join in. At halftime, squads perform a routine to entertain the crowd.

Many schools help cheerleaders pay for college. Most give **$500 to $1,000**. Harvard University offers **$22,000**.

Tryouts are often held in spring for the next school year.

Cheerleading Squads Athletes and Coaches

Squads are made up of different positions. Cheerleaders are prepared to fill any position. They know the special skills needed for each role. Cheerleaders usually focus on one position. It becomes their specialty. Bases are at the bottom of a stunt. It is their job to lift or throw the **flyer**. Flyers get thrown high up in the air. They do thrilling stunts. They have strong tumbling skills. **Spotters** must have good timing and focus. They help steady the stunt. Spotters make sure the flyer is caught safely.

For advanced stunts, a flyer is supported by two bases and two spotters.

Coaches are the leaders of cheerleading squads. They assign positions. Coaches keep the squad organized. They tell squads when to be at practices and games or competitions. Coaches teach skills, cheers, and routines. They make sure squads are practicing and performing safely.

Parents and guardians support and encourage squads with young members. They help them get to practices, games, and competitions on time. Some schools have a contract that parents and guardians must sign. They must promise to be positive and helpful.

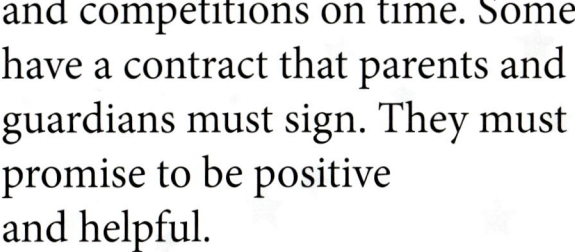

Many parents support squads by helping with hair and makeup, team activities, and special events.

The Right Tools

Squads spend most of their time in practice. They need a safe practice space. Special equipment helps them work safely.

Stunt Stepper A stunt stepper is a training device. Flyers use it to learn and practice balance before trying a stunt with a base. A University of Kentucky cheerleader invented the tool.

Trampoline Trampolines are used when learning jumps and tumbling. Long trampoline **runways** are used to practice stunts. Cheerleaders also practice balance on trampolines.

Hand Chalk During practice, cheerleaders must have a firm and steady grip. They rub hand chalk on their palms for extra grip. It soaks up the sweat from their hands. Hand chalk comes in powder and liquid form.

Practice Mat Practice mats protect cheerleaders. Jumps, tumbling, and handstands are all practiced on mats. They provide a stable base and landing area. This minimizes injury during practice.

The Right Moves

Squads practice until they can perform their moves perfectly. They trust each other to do all moves with accuracy and strength. Squads must work together during routines.

X-Out In an X-Out, cheerleaders do a jump with the knees held up to the chest. In the middle of the jump, the legs are untucked. The body forms an X with arms and legs outstretched. Cheerleaders then land with feet and legs together.

Pike Jump In a pike jump, cheerleaders keep their legs straight and together. They bring their legs up to their arms. Arms reach straight out. Cheerleaders bend at the waist and touch their toes. Their head is up.

Kick Twist Basket Toss

In a kick twist basket toss, bases throw a flyer straight up. While in the air, the flyer kicks one leg up. Then, he or she spins once around on the way down.

Bow and Arrow

In a bow and arrow, the flyer kicks one leg straight up next to the head. He or she holds the leg with the opposite hand. The other arm is in a T motion in front of the kicked-up leg.

Getting Involved

Cheerleaders are always part of a team. Squads work together at practice and performances. Do you think you have what it takes to be on a cheerleading squad?

Cheerleading is growing in the United Kingdom. New squads are forming every year.

1. Learn about the cheerleading squads in your area. Ask a cheerleader you know to tell you how to get started at school, or look up All-star squads online.

2. Get fit and eat healthily. All members of a cheerleading squad must be strong and healthy. Build up your **endurance** by running. Get stronger by working out.

3. Attend all practices and team events. A cheerleading squad spends time together both on and off the field. This is how they build friendships and trust. Be sure you have the time needed to be a **dependable** team member.

4. Be a good teammate. Have a good attitude. Cheerleaders are known for being positive and enthusiastic. This begins with being helpful to your squad.

EATING HEALTHILY

Healthy food gives cheerleaders the fuel their bodies need in practice and performance. Foods such as whole grain pasta and bread give energy. Fresh fruits and vegetables are healthy choices as well. Drinking water keeps cheerleaders **hydrated**. Athletes avoid eating too much sugar. Sugar in candy and soft drinks gives instant energy. It does not last. Cheerleaders should choose healthy foods for all their meals and snacks.

Prospect High Panthers

The Prospect High School Panthers is a squad in Saratoga, California. The squad helps younger students learn about the sport. Every year, it hosts a cheer **clinic**. The clinic raises money for the squad.

The clinic is held over three evenings. Students from kindergarten through eighth grade can sign up. Up to 60 students attend.

Almost 60 percent of children ages 6 to 12 participate in team sports. This includes cheerleading.

Many gyms and community centers offer cheerleading clinics.

Squad members help the students learn cheers. Each Panthers cheerleader works with three or four students. He or she teaches a routine. Then, the students perform the routine at a Prospect High School basketball game.

Panthers squad members bond with the younger cheerleaders. They form friendships. The cheerleaders often are **mentors**. Many of the students return to the clinic year after year.

Quiz

1 How many athletes do most squads have?

Between 5 and 36.

2 Were the first squads all female?

No, they were all male.

3 In which year did the Baltimore Colts form the first professional squad?

1954

4 How long do many tryouts last?

Three days

5 What are the three positions on a squad?

Base, flyer, and spotter

6 Who invented the stunt stepper?

A University of Kentucky cheerleader

7 How many times does the flyer spin during a kick twist basket toss?

Once

8 What are some examples of healthy foods?

Whole grain pasta and bread, fresh fruits, and vegetables

Key Words

All-star: a type of cheerleading in which athletes compete during routines that include advanced moves

championships: final competitions that determine the overall winner in a sport

clinic: a workshop or class on a single subject

dependable: able to be counted on and trusted

endurance: an ability to keep going when tired or stressed

flyer: a cheerleader who is held up or tossed into the air when doing stunts

hydrated: having enough water

mentors: people who are experienced and teach younger people

professional: a type of cheerleading in which athletes are paid for their work

runways: long, narrow paths or platforms

sideline: a type of cheerleading in which a team cheers on its sport team from the sides of the field

spotters: cheerleaders who watch flyers and catch them if they fall during stunts

stunts: advanced cheerleading moves during which cheerleaders are held up or tossed in the air

tryouts: events during which people are tested and judged in order to join a team or group

tumbling: gymnastics moves, such as somersaults, rolls, and leaps

Worlds: the biggest competition for All-star cheerleading; short for Cheerleading Worlds

Index

All-star 5, 7, 9, 19

Baltimore Colts 9, 22

coaches 11, 12, 13

endurance 19

flyer 12, 14, 17, 22

professional 5, 6, 9, 22
Prospect High School Panthers 20, 21

routines 4, 11, 13, 16, 21

spotters 12, 22
stunts 4, 8, 12, 14, 22

tryouts 11, 22

Warner, Pop 9

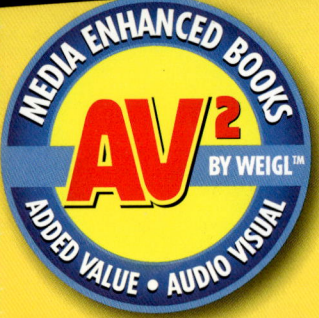

Log on to www.av2books.com

AV² by Weigl brings you media enhanced books that support active learning. Go to www.av2books.com, and enter the special code found on page 2 of this book. You will gain access to enriched and enhanced content that supplements and complements this book. Content includes video, audio, weblinks, quizzes, a slideshow, and activities.

AV² Online Navigation

Audio
Listen to sections of the book read aloud.

Book Pages
AV² pages directly correspond to pages in the book.

Video
Watch informative video clips.

Key Words
Study vocabulary, and complete a matching word activity.

Embedded Weblinks
Gain additional information for research.

Quizzes
Test your knowledge.

Slideshow
View images and captions, and prepare a presentation.

Try This!
Complete activities and hands-on experiments.

AV² was built to bridge the gap between print and digital. We encourage you to tell us what you like and what you want to see in the future.

Sign up to be an AV² Ambassador at www.av2books.com/ambassador.

Due to the dynamic nature of the internet, some of the URLs and activities provided as part of AV² by Weigl may have changed or ceased to exist. AV² by Weigl accepts no responsibility for any such changes. All media enhanced books are regularly monitored to update addresses and sites in a timely manner. Contact AV² by Weigl at 1-866-649-3445 or av2books@weigl.com with any questions, comments, or feedback.